MASTERS OF PHOTOGRAPHY

MATHEW BRADY

770 BRADY

7/99

OL

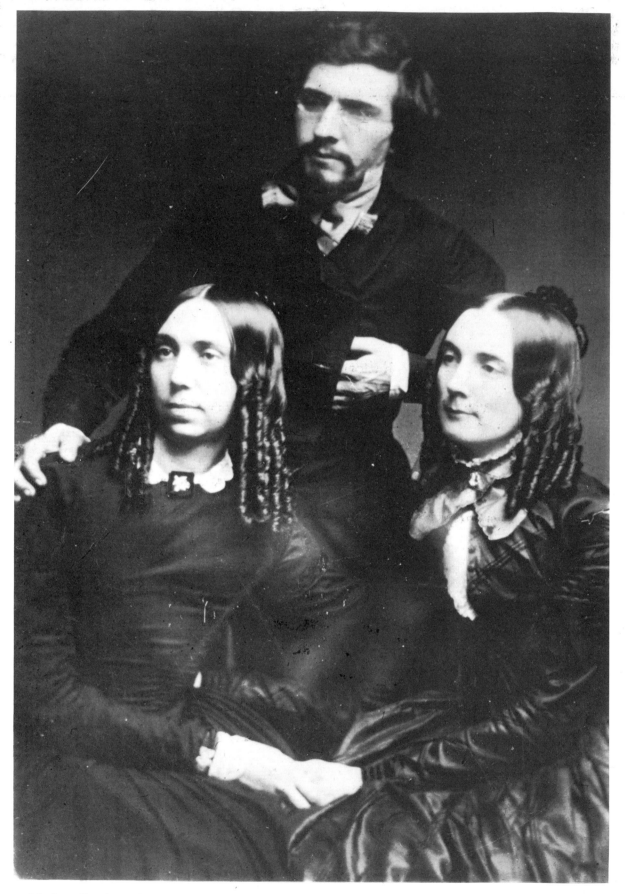

Mathew Brady, wife Julia Handy Brady and sister, 1896 (Library of Congress, Washington, DC)

MASTERS OF PHOTOGRAPHY

MATHEW BRADY

Text by George Hobart

Macdonald

A MACDONALD BOOK

© Macdonald & Co (Publishers) Ltd 1984

First published in Great Britain in 1984
by Macdonald & Co (Publishers) Ltd
London & Sydney

A member of BPCC plc

British Library Cataloguing in Publication Data
Hobart, George
    Mathew Brady.—(Masters of
    photography)
    1. Brady, Mathew B.
    I. Title   II. Series
    770'.92'4   TR140.B7

ISBN 0-356-10501-6

Filmset by
Text Filmsetters Ltd

Printed and bound in England by
The Alden Press
Oxford

Macdonald & Co (Publishers) Ltd
Maxwell House
74 Worship Street
London EC2A 2EN

Mathew B. Brady (no one ever knew what the B stood for) or Mr B., or Brady of Broadway, was as well-known as any famous man in his own time. His credit line, 'Photograph [or Daguerreotype] by Brady', was a hallmark of professional excellence as well as a popular trademark of bustling and energetic mid-nineteenth century America – an America teeming with professional photographers. An affable, industrious and ambitious self-made man. Brady's meteoric rise as a portrait photographer during the 1840s and 1850s paralleled the rise of the art, science and popularity of the medium.

Throughout his adult life Brady was plagued by the steady deterioration of his eyesight, from which he had suffered since childhood. By tireless work, determination, innovation and business acumen, however, he overcame his physical infirmity to become one of the greatest and most successful portrait photographers of all time. Yet in 1860, at the peak of commercial and artistic success, he sacrificed his fame, fortune and health in order to record for history the Great Civil War of 1861-5. Although his wife and friends urged him not to leave his immensely successful portrait business for the financial and physical risks of pictorial war documentation, he later said, 'A spirit in my feet said "Go", and I went.' The spirit and vision which made him one of the first photographic historians of famous men, women and events added to his artistry in portraiture to assure Brady's position as an acknowledged master of photography.

Little is known of Brady's early life and still less of his childhood. He said that he was born in Warren County, in the Lake George region of upstate New York, probably in 1823, and we know that he died in the alms ward of the New York City Presbyterian Hospital on 15 January 1896. Yet in between his birth and death, despite his fame, are many frustrating gaps about his adult life. One of his many biographers, James Horan, suggests that the lack of a personal diary or letters is due to the simple fact that Brady could not write.

As far as we know, Brady left his farm and home for nearby Saratoga at the age of sixteen where he learned to manufacture jewellery cases and where he became a friend of the portrait painter William Page. In the same year, 1839, the two young men went to New York City to seek their fortunes.

Brady's arrival in this bustling metropolitan centre of the arts coincided perfectly with the exciting news of the arrival of the daguerreotype. The daguerreotype, one of the first methods of capturing an image by chemical means, was a direct positive process, with no intermediate negative. A sheet of copper was plated with silver and thoroughly buffed and polished. The silver surface was then exposed to iodine vapour until silver iodide was formed on the exposed surface. The resulting sensitized plate was placed in a simple camera, where an image was formed on it by means of light admitted through the lens opening. The latent image was brought out by subsequent exposure to mercury vapour. The developed plate was then washed with hypo (hyposulphite of soda), rinsed with distilled water, dried and mounted under glass. The tool and its craftsman were quickly to meet when Page introduced Brady to his art teacher, Professor Samuel Finlay Breese Morse. Morse had been in Paris during the winter of 1838-9 to present his own invention – the telegraph – to the Academy of Sciences and on his return brought America her first knowledge of Louis Daguerre's wondrous invention.

At this time the process was still secret. It was not until 19 August, after the French Government had voted an annuity to the inventors (Daguerre and the heirs of his deceased partner, Nicéphore Niépce), that the process was made public and free to the world. At the time of their meeting Morse was trying to finance his recent invention while seeking to survive, as Brady recalled, by 'painting portraits at starvation prices', and by teaching the new science of daguerrean photography.

Poor, young Mathew Brady must have recognized immediately the financial and artistic potential of this exciting new career, whereby all one had to do was to build a camera, clean, polish and coat a sheet of copper, find a subject – and take his picture. Despite his progressively failing vision and lack of formal education, especially in chemistry, Brady plunged into his career as photographer.

America was a land of opportunity, and no young American was more opportunistic than he.

In order to earn the fifty-dollar tuition for Morse's school of daguerreotypy, Brady worked long hours as a clerk in A. T. Stewart's dry goods shop, while making miniature jewellery cases which were soon to be used to encase the exquisite gems of daguerrean art. His association with the eminent Morse brought him into contact with most of the pioneers of American photography, including John Plumbe, Edward Anthony, Samuel Broadbent, Albert Southworth, John Draper and Alexander Wolcott. During the years 1840-3 he worked and studied hard, experimenting with daguerreotypes until, in 1844, he opened Brady's Daguerrean Miniature Gallery. The location of the gallery was well chosen, being on the corner of Broadway and Fulton Street across from P. T. Barnum's American Museum. Success breeds success and, with a clientele that included most of the famous men and women of society, government and arts and letters, acclaim came to Brady almost immediately and his business grew at a phenomenal rate.

Brady was always dedicated to professional excellence – and to history: 'The camera is the eye of history,' he said. 'You must never make bad pictures'. Looking back on his career, he recalled that 'from the first I regarded myself as under obligation to my country to preserve the faces of its historic men and mothers'. He tirelessly sought to make as complete and true a record as possible of all the great personages of his time – including the grand old men who were unable or unwilling to come to his studio. He recalled how, in 1845, he 'sent to the Hermitage and had Andrew Jackson taken barely in time to save his aged lineaments to posterity'. Most of the famous, however, readily presented themselves to Brady's Broadway Valhalla, as the Fulton Street gallery was known.

Although he sought to preserve the famous in portraiture, Brady also found time for the infamous. In 1844 he travelled with Eliza Farnham, matron of Sing-Sing prison, to Blackwell's Island prison and to the Long Island Farm School. Mrs Farnham used nineteen of Brady's daguerreotypes of the inmates as published wood-engravings, describing him as having shown 'indefatigable patience with a

class of the most difficult of all sitters'.

In 1850 Brady at last realized his ambition when the *Gallery of Illustrious Americans* was published, a five-pound, thirty-dollar, elegantly bound book 'containing portraits of twelve of the most eminent citizens of the American Republic since the days of Washington, all from the original daguerreotypes taken by Brady'. The book was acclaimed but was much too expensive for popular distribution. Why should one look at twelve lithographic copies of daguerreotypes at home when one could experience the thrill of going in person to Brady's Portrait Gallery?

What an experience it must have been for anyone – especially an American living in that patriotic period of Manifest Destiny – to look with awe and reverence at the faces of American history and culture that lined the walls of Brady's gallery! Brady's own joy was diminished only by the sorrow he felt at not having had a camera to record the faces of the Founding Fathers, and even of antiquity. As the famed journalist George Albert Townsend lamented, 'For want of such art as his [Brady's] we worship the Jesus of the painters, not knowing the face of our Redeemer'.

The year 1850 came to an exciting conclusion for the daguerrean world with Queen Victoria's announcement that the first World's Fair was to be held in London the following spring. Photography was to be one of the major categories of international competition, which prompted intense activity among daguerrean artists the world over. In competition with the many outstanding American daguerreotypists, Brady had won numerous awards, but none as prestigious as the top prize which was to be his at the great Crystal Palace Exhibition of 1851. The official jury report heaped praise upon American daguerrean artistry, especially that of Brady.

Having shipped his precious selection of forty-eight portraits across the Atlantic in advance, Brady took the first real holiday of his working life when he left New York with his young wife Julia in July 1851 for a lengthy trip to England and the Continent. His trip, however, was not entirely one of rest and relaxation, as he captured the likenesses of many of the great men of Europe, for whom it was

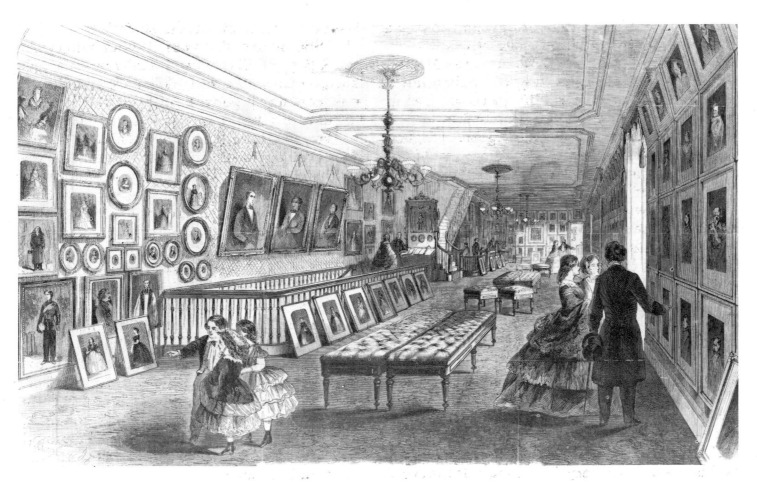

Mathew Brady's new photographic gallery, 1861 (Library of Congress, Washington, DC)

a pleasure to be daguerreotyped by Brady.

While in London Brady observed the collodion, or so-called wet-plate, process, newly invented by the Englishman Frederick Scott Archer. The wet-plate process was revolutionary in that it could produce a good glass-plate negative from which an unlimited number of paper prints could be made. The process had been made possible by the discovery of a new compound called collodion, a thick, syrupy mixture of alcohol, ether, and nitrated cotton that was coated evenly over one side of a glass plate. Because alcohol and ether quickly evaporate, a thin transparent film remained on the glass which, when bathed in a silver nitrate solution, caused the light-sensitive compound silver iodide to collect upon the collodion film surface. The plate then had to be exposed in the camera and then developed in less than an hour while still wet or damp or else its sensitivity was lost (hence the name wet-plate, which is given to the collodion

process). In learning the new process Brady did not immediately recognize that it would soon spell the doom of his daguerrean art; in the meantime he laid the foundation for a future business and artistic relationship with the Scotsman Alexander Gardner — a master of the new wet-plate photography.

Brady returned to New York in May 1852 refreshed and recharged with the energy needed to deal with the many radical changes that were to occur in the photography business. And big, competitive business it had become, especially in New York City where in 1853 there were more professional daguerreotypists than in all of England.

Brady was obsessed with the task of outfitting his newest gallery at 359 Broadway with the most lavish and expensive furnishings and equipment in order to attract the fashionable patronage away from the daguerrean palaces of his Broadway competitors. A French visitor wrote, 'everything is here united to distract the mind of the visitor from his cares and give to his countenance an expression of calm contentment. The merchant, the physician, the lawyer, the manufacturer, even the restless politician, here forget their labours. Surrounded thus, how is it possible to hesitate at the cost of a portrait?'

By 1853 fierce competition and the standardization of photographic processes had halved the cost of daguerrean portraits. The popular $2\frac{3}{4} \times 3\frac{1}{4}$-inch daguerreotype at Brady's or at his chief competitor's palaces cost two dollars or more, despite the fact that hundreds of cheap operators in the city were charging as little as twenty-five cents. Brady advertised his concern for the state of the art in the New York newspapers:

> ... Being unwilling to abandon any artistic ground to the producers of inferior work, I have no fear in appealing to an enlightened public as to their choice. ... I wish to vindicate true art, and leave the community to decide whether it is best to encourage real excellence or its opposite; to preserve and perfect an art, or permit it to degenerate by inferiority of materials which must correspond with the meanness of the price.   M.B. Brady.

But Brady's appeal to an enlightened public was in vain; a eulogy to his beloved Daguerrean Art, whose palaces would soon be renamed Photographic. In *The Photographic Art Journal* Snelling reported to his readers that by March 1854 more collodion process apparatus and supplies had been 'sold in the United States within the last three months ... than during the whole previous time since its discovery [in 1851]. ... In view of the hosts of 25-cent galleries springing up in all quarters, our most respectable artists begin to look to the crystallotype [an early collodion type] to redeem their artistic skill from the odium cast upon the daguerrean art by its prostitution to such paltry results.' The best and most practical artists, Brady, Gurney and Lawrence, had already begun to put aside their daguerrean apparatus to become fledgling students of the new art of the collodion wet-plate. (Many types of the new collodion process were popular in the United States from 1854 to 1860. The ambro-type, for example, a photographic negative on glass, held the public fancy until 1857 when it was supplanted by a profusion of paper processes.)

There is evidence that from this time on Brady spent less time behind the camera. The business of supervising the operation of two large galleries in New York and a third in Washington, DC would be more than a full-time job for any man, and Brady's eyesight was deteriorating and the lenses in his spectacles became thicker and thicker. As early as 1851, *The Photographic and Fine Art Journal* pronounced that he was 'not an operator himself, a failing eyesight precluding the possibility of his using the camera with any certainty'. This statement is certainly contradicted by the evidence of the thousands of exposures definitely made by Brady over the next forty years.

In 1856 the Scotsman Alexander Gardner came to New York, bringing not only an expert knowledge of the collodion processes but also his skill in making paper enlargements from small negatives. Brady's introduction of the imperial photograph captured public fancy as well as sizeable fees from the elite, who could afford the 14×17 or 17×20-inch portraits. Other photographers tried to produce still larger photographs up to and beyond life-size, the imperfections of these gigantic enlargements being reduced or removed by artful retouching. While Brady did not venture beyond the exquisite imperial size, he did produce three life-size portraits of Webster, Clay, and Calhoun from daguerreotypes which he had made in 1849 and 1850. The enlargements, made from wet-plate copy negatives, were finished in oils by John Neagle and Henry Darby. These beautiful portraits hung prominently in the New York gallery and now hang in the Senate Wing of the US Capitol. Brady, however, did have the last word on the bigness craze: in the autumn of 1858 he joined in celebrating the completion of the transatlantic cable by decorating the front of his gallery with a colossal transparency that contained portraits of Franklin, Morse and Field, measured 25×50 feet ($7\frac{1}{2} \times 15$ metres), and was illuminated from behind by six hundred candles!

In that same year Brady established a permanent gallery in Washington, DC, with Alexander Gardner as manager. Another studio had been established there previously in 1847, its greatest success having been to bring together Brady and the lovely young Julia Handy, his beloved wife and partner for nearly forty years.

At this time a paper process came into vogue which remained immensely popular for the next fifty years. Stereoscopic photography was based on the optical principle that the slightly different images seen by two human eyes are combined in the brain to produce the sensory illusion of relief and perspective. Brady later used this three-dimensional quality to bring the horrors of the Civil War vividly to the viewers of his stereo cards.

Another collodion paper process that became very popular in 1860 was the *carte-de-visite*, a 2⅛ × 3½-inch portrait print mounted on a slightly larger card which was used as a calling card or souvenir memento. These were produced by the millions through 1866 and constituted the only profitable side of Brady's business during that period. The impact of these inexpensive little cards is illustrated by the story behind Brady's famous Cooper Union portrait of Abraham Lincoln. Lincoln went to New York in February 1860 to address the congregation at Henry Ward Beecher's church in Brooklyn but was advised, for better political exposure, to speak instead at the Cooper Institute in Manhattan. Furthermore, he was urged by his Republican hosts to have his portrait made by Brady, even though the latter was a Tammany Democrat and a supporter of Stephen Douglas.

In 1860 Lincoln was little-known or liked east of Illinois. His reputation was that of a coarse, clumsy, ungainly country-bumpkin. Brady's *carte-de-visite* portrait shows him as Honest Abe, with a face and stature of strength, dignity, and calm determination. The cards were immediately sold in vast quantity to the public, while newspapers reproduced the portrait in wood-engraving, and Currier & Ives as lithographs. Later, when Brady was introduced to Lincoln at the White House, the President was quick to acknowledge that 'Brady and the Cooper Institute made me President'.

Less than two weeks after the Lincoln portrait, Brady moved uptown to an even more elegant and spacious gallery at the corner of 10th Street and Broadway. The press once more tried to top one another with superlatives to describe its elegance. As one reporter wrote: 'If Brady lived in England his gallery would be called the Royal Gallery.' Brady's gallery indeed became the Royal Gallery and he the Royal Photographer when, in October 1860, the Prince of Wales paid a surprise visit. Although many New York photographers had vied for the Prince's attention, he chose Brady without invitation or solicitation. After 'inspecting with curious interest the portraits of the statesmen and the other celebrities of his country', the prince willingly posed for a variety of portraits. Brady politely asked to what he owed the honour of the Royal presence, and was answered: 'Are you not the Mr Brady who earned the prize nine years ago in London? You owe it to yourself. We had your place of business down in our notebooks before we started.'

Eighteen months later an American correspondent wrote of the large photography exhibit in London that Brady was the 'best and best-known expert in this modern and money-making art... for I have never seen anything in London or Paris superior, if equal... to those done under the practiced hand of Brady'. In April 1862, however, photography was for Mr B neither money-making nor art. With the inexorable approach of the conflict between North and South, Brady had committed himself totally, financially and physically, to the historical photo-documentation of the bitter and bloody war between the Union and the Confederacy.

His baptism under fire came on 21 July 1861 at the first major battle of the war, just twenty-three miles from the nation's capital near the town of Manassas, Virginia and less than one hundred miles northwest of the Confederate capital of Richmond. Brady recalled, 'I went to the first battle of Bull Run with two wagons.... We stayed all night at Centreville; we got as far as Blackbourne's Ford; we made pictures and expected to be in Richmond next day, but it was not so, and so our apparatus was a good deal damaged on the way back to Washington'. Contemporary accounts show Brady to have been overly modest in appraising his harrowing experience and contribution to history. *Humphrey's Journal* states:

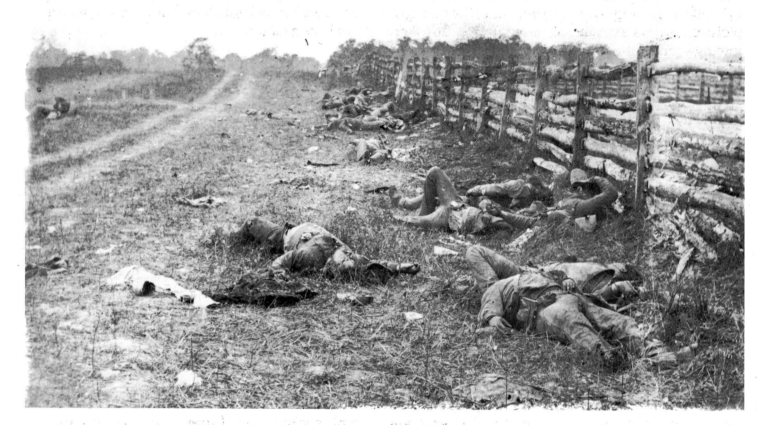

Dead as they fell at Antietam, Maryland, 17 September 1862 (Library of Congress, Washington, DC)

... Brady has shown more pluck than many of the officers and soldiers.... He went ... with his sleeves tucked up and his big camera directed upon every point of interest on the field ... this collection is the most curious and interesting we have ever seen. The groupings of entire regiments and divisions, within a space of a couple of feet square, present some .... Considering the circumstances under which they were taken, amidst the excitement, the rapid movements ... there is nothing to compare with them....'

After the crushing defeat of an ill-prepared Union army, it must have been clear to Brady, as well as to all Northerners, that the road to Richmond would be long and costly in time, men and material. Yet Brady of Broadway, the rich and fashionable por-

trait photographer, set to work immediately to hire and equip a staff of excellent photographers and to send them into the field. Brady undertook an enormous expense in supervising, supplying and paying a staff of up to twenty men scattered over a great many battlefronts and he and his field photographers worked under extremely difficult conditions. Because the wet-plate was the only photographic process available at the time, a darkroom and all necessary supplies — glass plates of many sizes, collodion, silver nitrate and developer, as well as a variety of cumbersome cameras — had to be carried with the photographer at all times. In order to do this Brady had large wagons modified to serve as portable darkrooms. These were affectionately called 'Whatsit' wagons by the Union soldiers, whose curiosity soon grew to respect for the men who risked life and limb to follow them into battle.

Following armies anywhere in their portable darkroom wagons – jolting across the worst imaginable terrain with hundreds of glass plates and bottles of chemicals – was a miraculous endeavour in itself and having arrived at the scene, the taking of pictures seems even more miraculous. If the following scenario seems complex, it should only add to our wonder at the accomplishments of Brady and his staff. A team of two photographers would arrive at the scene which they wished to record. One would carefully mix a gun cotton solution with equal amounts of sulfuric ether and alcohol to form the collodion, which was then iodized by adding iodide of potassium and potassium bromide. The collodion was poured evenly on to a clean plate of glass and the ether and alcohol allowed a few minutes to evaporate. The coated plate was then sensitized by immersion, in total darkness, in a bath solution of silver nitrate. The sensitized plate was then put into a holder and inserted immediately into a camera, which had already been set up, aimed and focused by the other member of the team. Exposure and developing had to be done within a few minutes, especially in the warm, humid weather of the South (only in extremely cold weather could there be as much as an hour delay). Uncapping the lens for the necessary exposure of up to thirty seconds meant that no action could ever be captured. The exposed plate was then rushed back to the darkroom wagon for developing in a mixture of water and acetic and pyrogallic acids, and then washed in a solution of hypo – sulphate of soda or cyanide of potassium. Only then could the plate be washed, dried and put away.

J. Pitcher Spencer, a photographer who accompanied one of Brady's tours, reminisced in 1912:

We worked long with one of the foremost of Brady's men, and here let me doff my hat to the name of M. B. Brady – few today are worthy to carry his camera case, even as far as ability from the photographic standpoint goes .... When I made some views, there came a realization of some of the immense difficulties surmounted by those who made war pictures. When you realize that the most sensitive of all the list of chemicals are requisite to make collodion, which must coat every plate, and that the very slightest breath might carry enough 'poison' across the plate being coated to make it produce a blank spot ... you may have perhaps a faint idea of the care requisite to produce a picture....

Brady, quite obviously, could not be the general of his widespread army of cameramen and aim and fire their photographic weapons himself, even if his poor eyesight permitted. As director of this huge operation, which he likened to 'a rich newspaper' and for which he 'had men in all parts of the army', he himself was able to take only a few hundred of the ten thousand wet-plate exposures produced under his direction. After Bull Run he was at Antietam, Maryland, and Fredericksburg, Gettysburg and Petersburg, Virginia between 1862 and the end of the war in 1865, often under fire. In the autumn of 1862, Oliver Wendell Holmes searched through the unburied dead on the fields of Antietam in the hope and fear of finding the body of his son, whom he believed to have died in that terrible battle. He wrote in July 1863:

The field of photography is extending itself to embrace subjects of strange and sometimes of fearful interest.... We have now before us a series of photographs showing the field of Antietam.... These terrible mementos of one of the most sanguinary conflicts of the war we owe to the enterprise of Mr Brady of New York. We ourselves were on the field upon the Sunday following the Wednesday when the battle took place. It is not, however, for us to bear witness to the fidelity of views which the truthful sunbeam has delineated in all their dread reality. The photographs bear witness to the accuracy of some of our own sketches.... Let him who wishes to know what the war is look at this series of illustrations. These wrecks of manhood thrown together in careless heaps or ranged in ghastly rows for burial were alive but yesterday.... Many people would not look through this series. Many, having seen it and dreamed of its horrors, would lock it up in some secret drawer.

Holmes's view foretold the fate of Brady's complete photographic history of the war once the hostilities ceased: the truth of the war was too much to bear for those who had suffered through those four horrible years. Brady had gambled his fortune on the naive hope of recouping his expenses by selling sets of his prints to the public and a set of his negatives to a Federal archive. But the people wanted to forget the war, and the Government, which had not provided a penny to Brady, was now too concerned with the massive problems of the reconstruction of the South to give a thought to Brady and his collection.

Mathew B. Brady slipped into quiet obscurity. To pay off the E. & H.T. Anthony Company, his principal supplier and creditor, he gave them an entire set of his precious Civil War negatives and from 1869 to 1871 sought in vain to sell the rest to the US Government. It was not until 1875, after his New York gallery and properties had been sold to satisfy creditors and his negatives auctioned to pay their storage fee, that Congress finally voted an appropriation to Brady for the rights to the collection.

Only Brady's Washington DC gallery remained, operated by Levin C. Handy, Brady's nephew. Brady quietly continued to make photographs as and when his failing eyesight and general ill-health permitted. Alexander Gardner and Timothy O'Sullivan, his most famous former assistants, both died in 1882, and the death of his beloved Julia in 1887 left him alone and dispirited. A famous interview with George Alfred Townsend in *The New York World* in 1891 temporarily brought him back to public awareness. The account begins: 'Brady the photographer alive? The man who daguerreotyped Mrs. Alexander Hamilton and Mrs. Madison, Gen. Jackson, and Edgar A. Poe, Taylor's Cabinet, and old Booth? Thought he was dead many a year.'

On 30 April 1896 Brady was to be honoured at the opening of an exhibition of his war scenes at Carnegie Hall. But the honour came fifteen days too late. Mathew B. Brady died on 15 April alone and virtually penniless, in the alms ward of New York Presbyterian Hospital. An old friend gathered together his few personal effects, including his beloved ivory-handled cane which had been given to him by the Prince of Wales in 1860 when Brady was world-famous as the photographer of presidents and princes. His body was sent to Arlington National Cemetery for its final resting place among the great Americans and the faceless Civil War dead, whose deeds live forever in the art and vision of Mathew B. Brady.

Each of the twenty-five plates in this book has been printed from negatives or daguerreotypes which are in four major Brady collections. As I tried to select among several thousand choices and pondered the tens of thousands more which have been lost to view, except for book illustrations and written description, I often asked myself, what was the secret of Brady's success? How was he able to induce so many important people – from impatient politicians to irascible artists – to sit for up to two hours for half-a-dozen long exposures? How was he able to capture the true character traits of his celebrated sitters? Those great men and women who sat for his camera were put at ease because of Brady's personal charm, geniality, impeccable manners, and intelligent conversation. In explaining his success in capturing the cantankerous and camera-shy James Fenimore Cooper, Brady recalled, 'Perhaps my diffidence helped me out with genuine men'. He could be aggressively persuasive if necessary, witness his determination to find and photograph General Robert E. Lee only days after the close of the Civil War. 'It was supposed that after his defeat it would be preposterous to ask him to sit, but I thought that to be the time for the historical picture.' Lee reluctantly sat for six negatives on 17 April 1865 which are considered to be the finest portraits of him.

'The world will little note nor long remember what we say here – but it can never forget what they did here.' So said Abraham Lincoln at Gettysburg five months after the titanic struggle. Lincoln's thoughts, expressed on that historic day, may have been influenced by Brady's stereographic scenes of that battlefield. As Brady's portrait helped to make Lincoln President, so, too, has his art given immortality to other great men, women and events.

FRAMING AND MOUNTING

There are a number of ways to display photographs, depending on your personal taste, the picture itself, your initiative and the amount you wish to spend. The simplest method is to use ready-to-assemble framing kits, which will only take about 10 minutes of your time; but if you want a truly professional look, you might wish to mount or mat your photographs and then have them framed — or do it yourself.

Mounting

Like any kind of print or drawing, a photograph must be secured to a stiff surface before it is framed to keep the picture flat and to keep it from slipping about inside the frame. There are a wide variety of mounting boards available, in many colours and thicknesses, or weights, so it is best to go to an art shop, tell the assistant what you need and look through their stock. Remember, if the photograph is large you will not want the board to be so heavy that when the picture is framed it falls off the wall!

There are three mounting techniques: dry, adhesive and wet. Dry mounting should be left to a professional (most photographic processing firms offer such services) because it requires a special press, but the other two methods can be done easily at home.

Adhesive mounting

You will need a sheet of glass slightly larger than your mount to use as a weight; a soft cloth or rubber roller (4-6 in/10-5 cm) and a wide brush. When choosing the adhesive avoid rubber solutions because they lose their adhesiveness when they dry; spray adhesives (which can be bought in any art shop) are quick and less messy — test the spray on a piece of paper before you begin to gauge its density. Sheets of adhesive are also available but require a perfect eye and steady hand. If you feel confident, they are an easy way to mount a picture. Tape should not be used except as a temporary measure.

First calculate where the picture is to lie on the board and lightly tick the four corners with a pencil or prick them with a pin. Read the manufacturer's instructions on the adhesive and then apply it to the back of your print. Carefully position the print on the front of the mounting board and smooth out any wrinkles with the roller or cloth, working from the centre outwards.

Because the mount will tend to warp as the adhesive dries, the picture must be counter-mounted. Cut a piece of heavy brown craft paper the same size as the mount. Lightly dampen one side of the paper with clean water, apply adhesive to the other side and then secure it to the back of the mounting board. As the paper dries, it will counter-act the drying action of the photograph. Place the picture and mount under the sheet of glass until completely dry.

Wet mounting

Wet mounting is used for creased, torn or very old photographs. Immerse the photograph in clean water and place it face down on a sheet of glass. Using a brush or roller, carefully smooth the surface and apply a thin coat of adhesive to the back of the picture and to the mounting board. Put the picture on the board and gently press out any bubbles. Countermount the board (see above). Check the photograph for any wrinkles or bubbles and smooth out. Let the adhesive dry until it is just moist and place the mounted photograph under the sheet of glass and let dry completely.

Block mounting

This is especially effective for large photographs and means that no frame is needed. Self-adhesive commercial blocks are available in standard sizes but tend to be expensive. To make your own you will need a piece of mounting board about ⅜ in (9 mm) smaller than the print on all sides; cellulose adhesive, a brush, lots of newspaper, a soft cloth or rubber roller, a large piece of card, a sharp craft knife, a cutting mat and piece of fine glasspaper.

Mix enough cellulose adhesive to cover the print and the board (the board will absorb the first few coats, so make a lot). Soak the photograph in clean water for about 20 minutes. Place several layers of newspaper on your work surface and place the mounting board on top. Apply the adhesive to the back of the board in two applications. Remove your print from the water, let any water drip off and place it picture-side down on the work surface and cover the back with adhesive. Then position it carefully on the board, picture-side up. Using the soft cloth or roller, carefully push out any bubbles or wrinkles from the centre outwards. When dry, put the mounted print picture-side down on a piece of clean card (do not use newspaper or paper, which may damage the print). Put some heavy books evenly on top as a weight and let dry thoroughly (this can take up to two days.) When dry, put the board picture-side down on a cutting mat and, using a sharp knife, trim the excess edges of the print to the edges of the mounting board. Smooth the edges of the board (not the print) with glasspaper. Paint the edges of the board or leave neutral.

Matting

A mat can change any photograph into something quite stunning. It will require a certain amount of experimenting to determine what size border around your picture looks best: some photographs are heightened by having a very wide border, others need almost none at all. In all cases, however, it looks best to have the bottom border slightly wider than the other three. As well, there is a vast range of colours of board to choose from, so think these things through before you buy your supplies. Remember that the mat should never overwhelm the picture, but should simply enhance it.

You will need a very sharp craft knife, metal straightedge and steel tape, large or set square, cutting mat and sharp pencil.

First measure the board to make sure that it is square (the right angles at the corners should be exactly 90 degrees) and trim if necessary. The aperture, or opening, for your picture should overlap the print by about $\frac{1}{8}$ in (3 mm) all round. You can mark this on the board either in pencil or with pin-pricks at the corners. If marking with pencil, do so on the back of the board and cut from the back as well so that the marks will not show.

Before you begin cutting, it is a good idea to practise using the knife and straightedge, which can be tricky for the uninitiated, especially on the corners. Position the blade of the knife at either a 90-degree (for a vertical edge) or 45-degree (for a bevelled edge) angle to the straightedge. Draw the blade firmly and slowly from corner to corner. Avoid stopping, as this will produce a ragged edge, and be careful not to gather speed and overshoot the corners. When all four sides have been cut, lift the centre out. Use glasspaper to neaten the edges.

The mat can now be secured to the mount with adhesive. To make a permanent bond, coat both the mount and the mat with adhesive, let dry and then press together. For a less permanent bond, apply adhesive to only one surface. Your picture is now ready for framing.

Frameless Frames

Photographs can be displayed most effectively without frames to detract from them. There are many types of frameless frames available in standard sizes, from 8×10 in (18×24 cm) to 24×32 in (50×70 cm). Most are easily obtained from art shops — your only decision is the size you need and the amount you wish to spend. If you prefer, you can easily make your own. You will need mounting board, a mat, glass or acrylic, and clips or brackets. There are, again, a wide variety of clips and brackets available. The least obtrusive are known as Swiss clips. Whichever you choose, make sure they will fit the width of the mount, print, mat and glass.

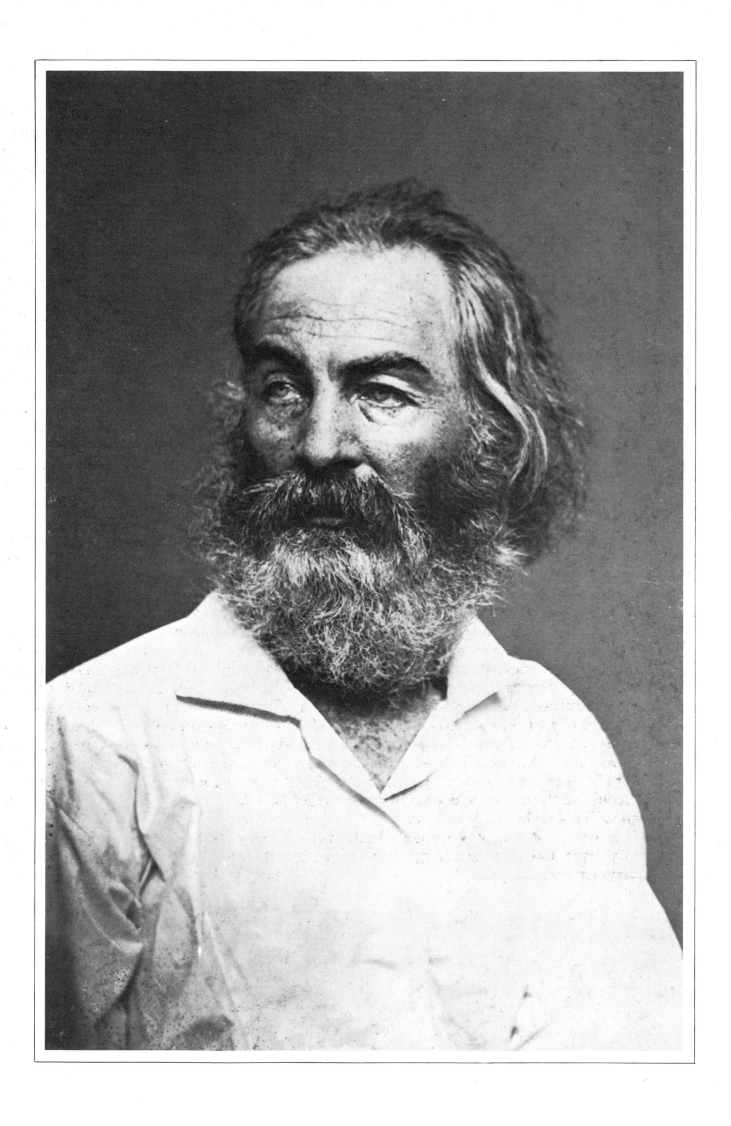

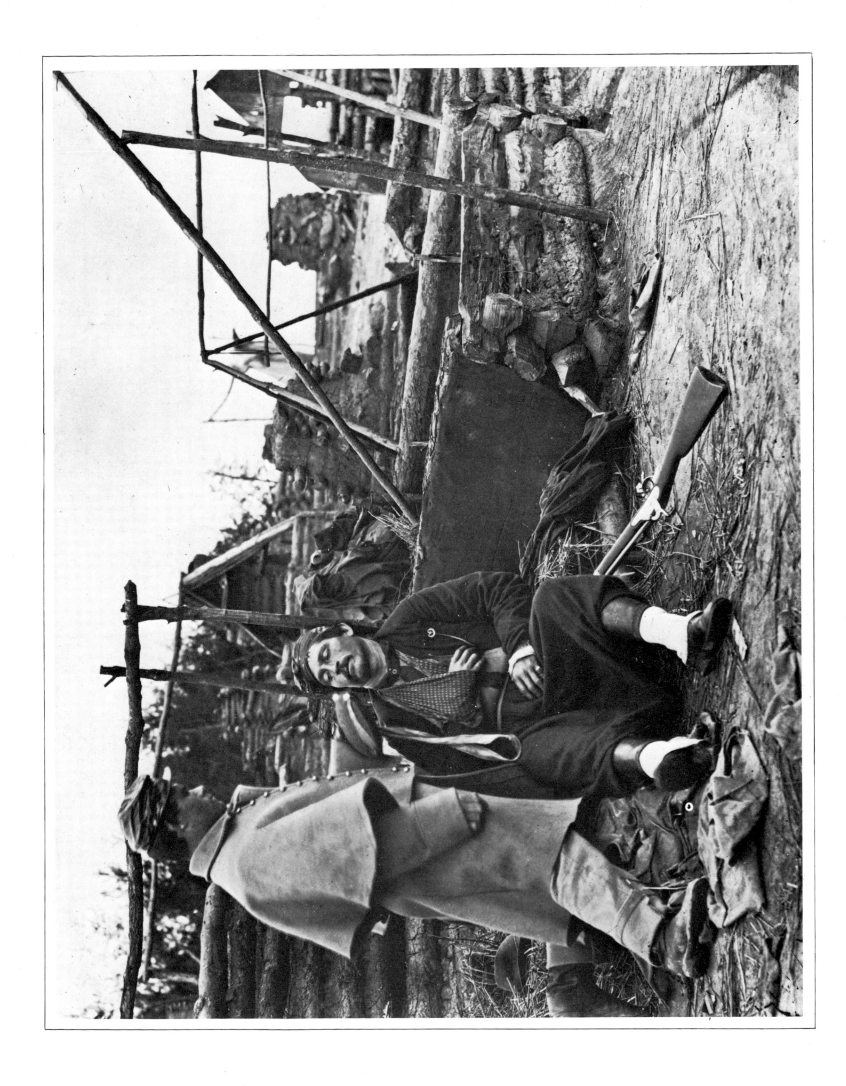

Scene showing deserted camp and wounded soldier (National Archives, Washington, DC)

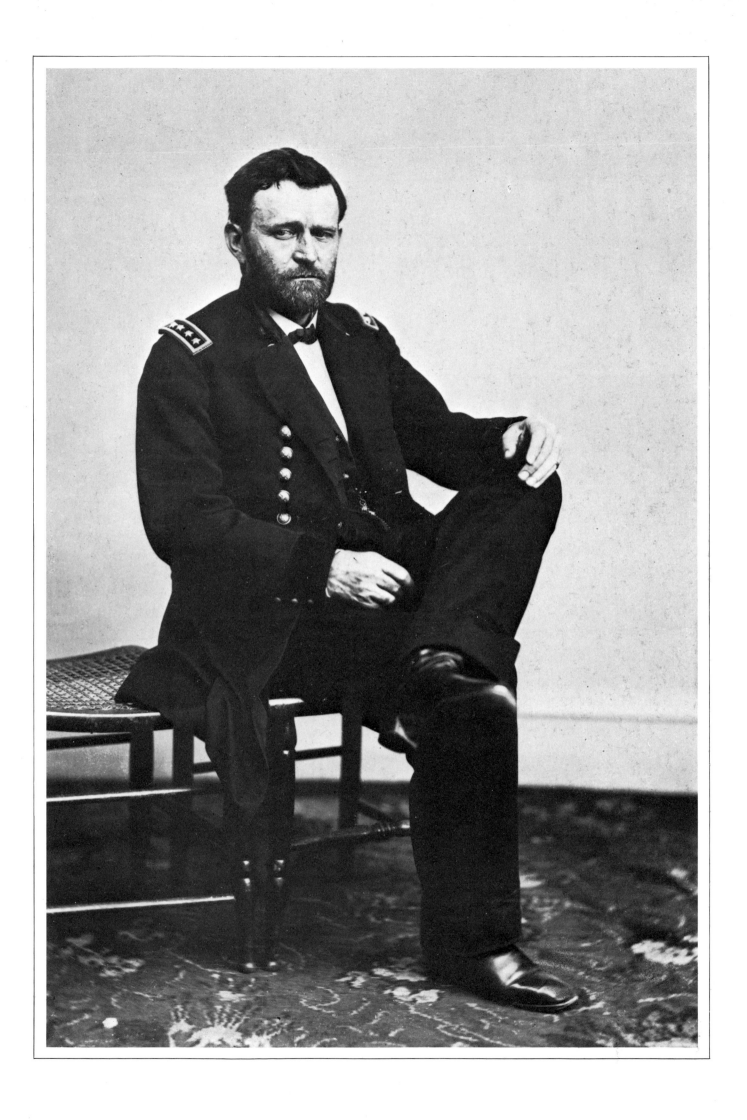

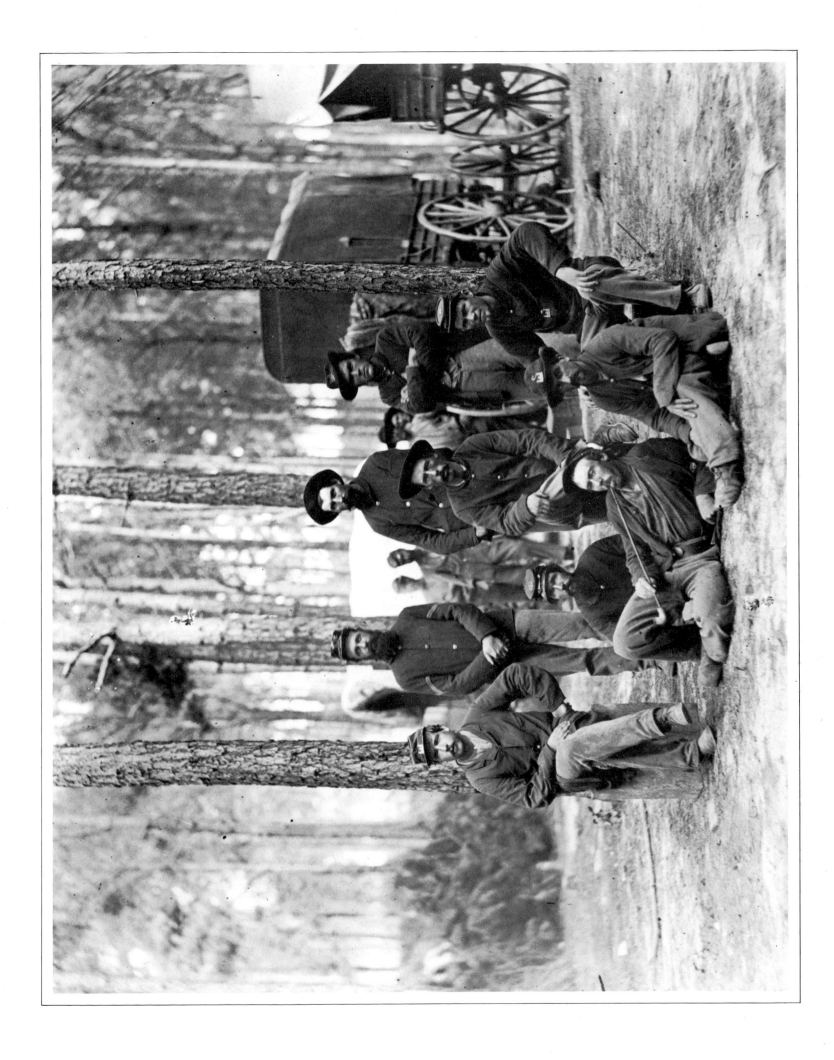

Group of Company B, US Engineer Battalion, Petersburg, Virginia, 1864 (Library of Congress, Washington, DC)

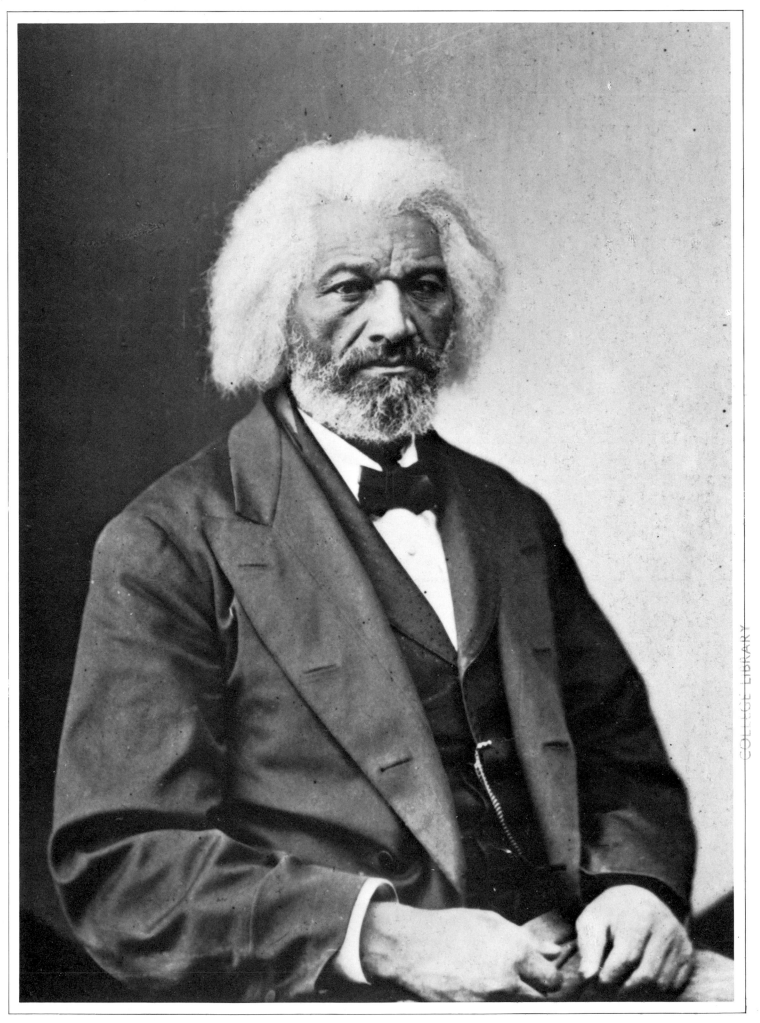

Frederick Douglass (Library of Congress, Washington, DC)

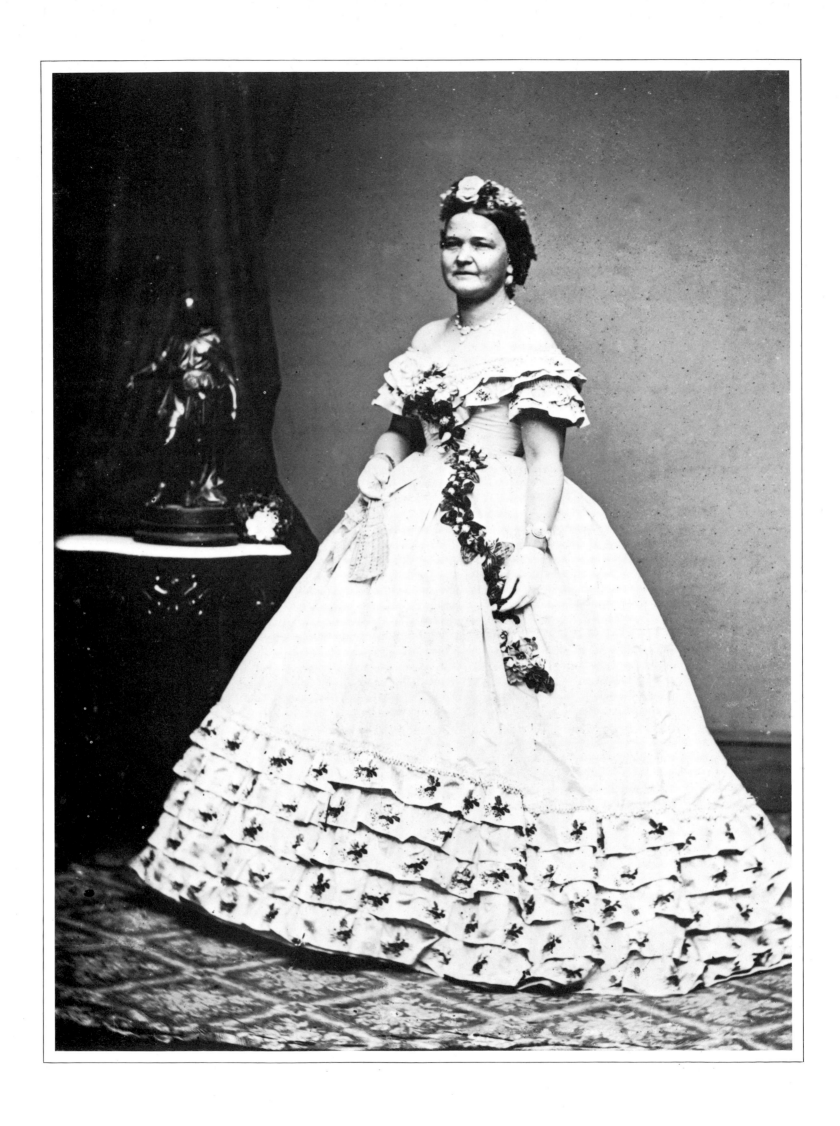

Mary Todd Lincoln, 1861 (Library of Congress, Washington, DC)

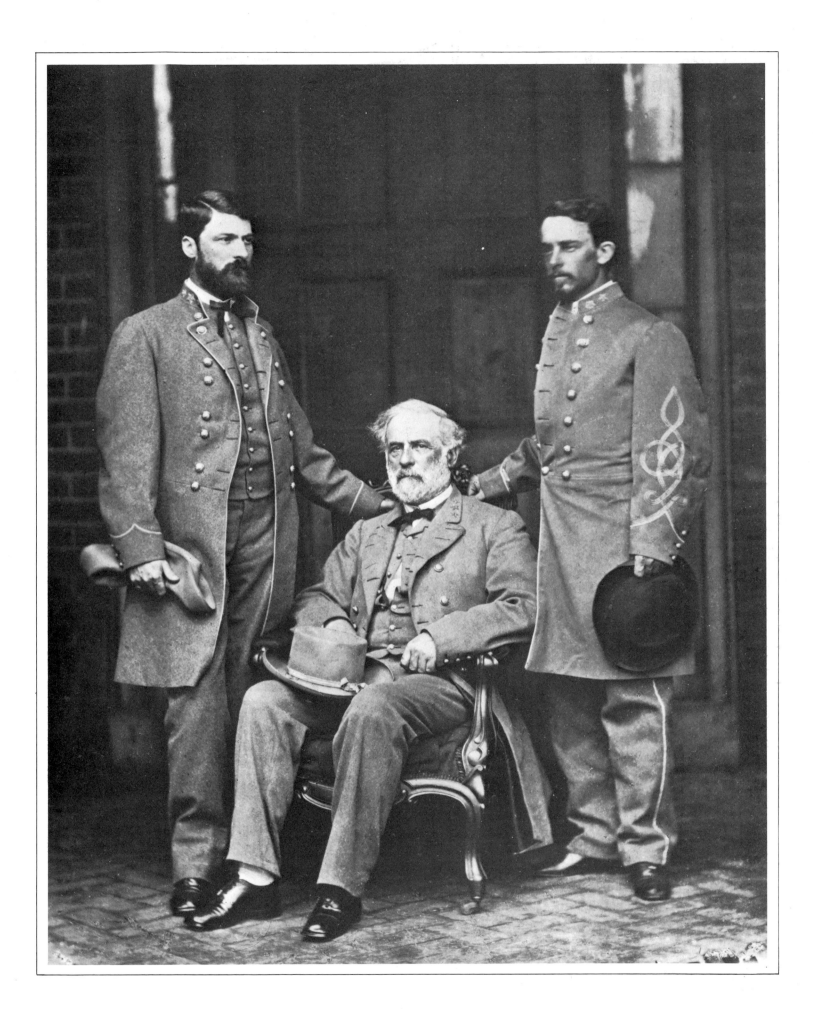

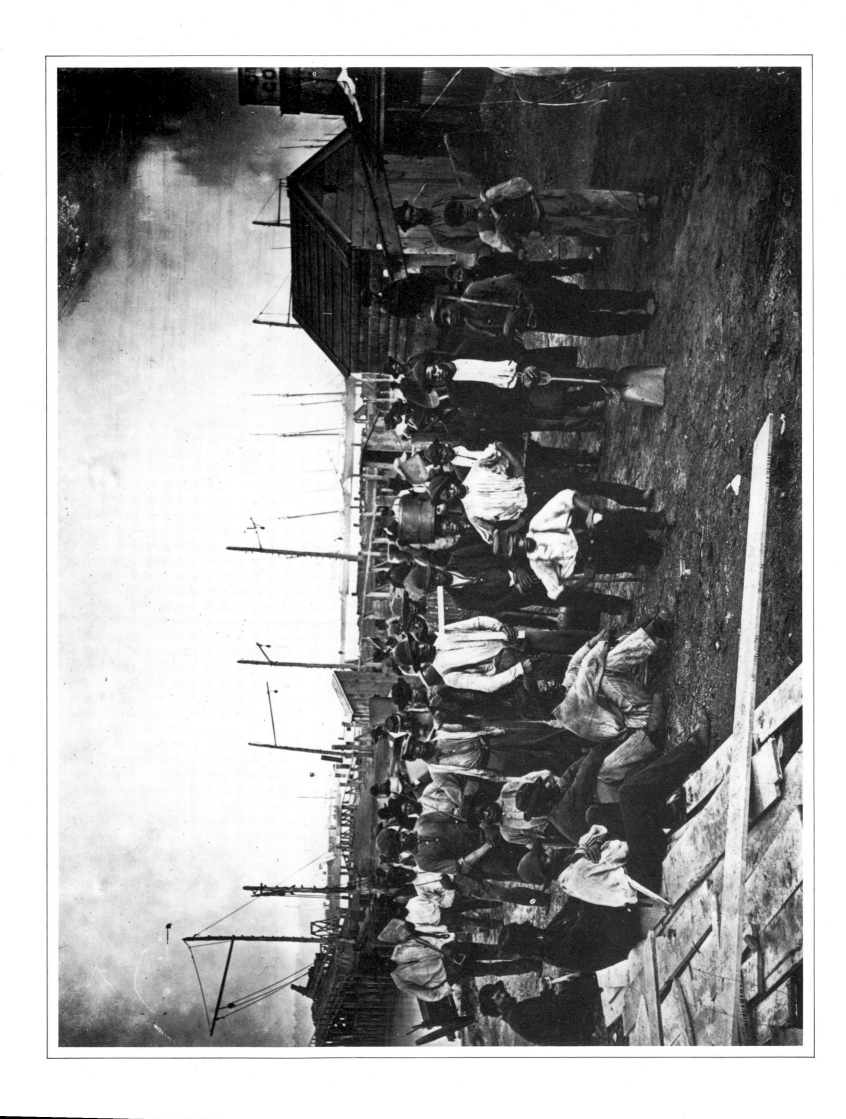

Black labourers on a wharf on the James River, c. 1864 (National Archives, Washington, DC)

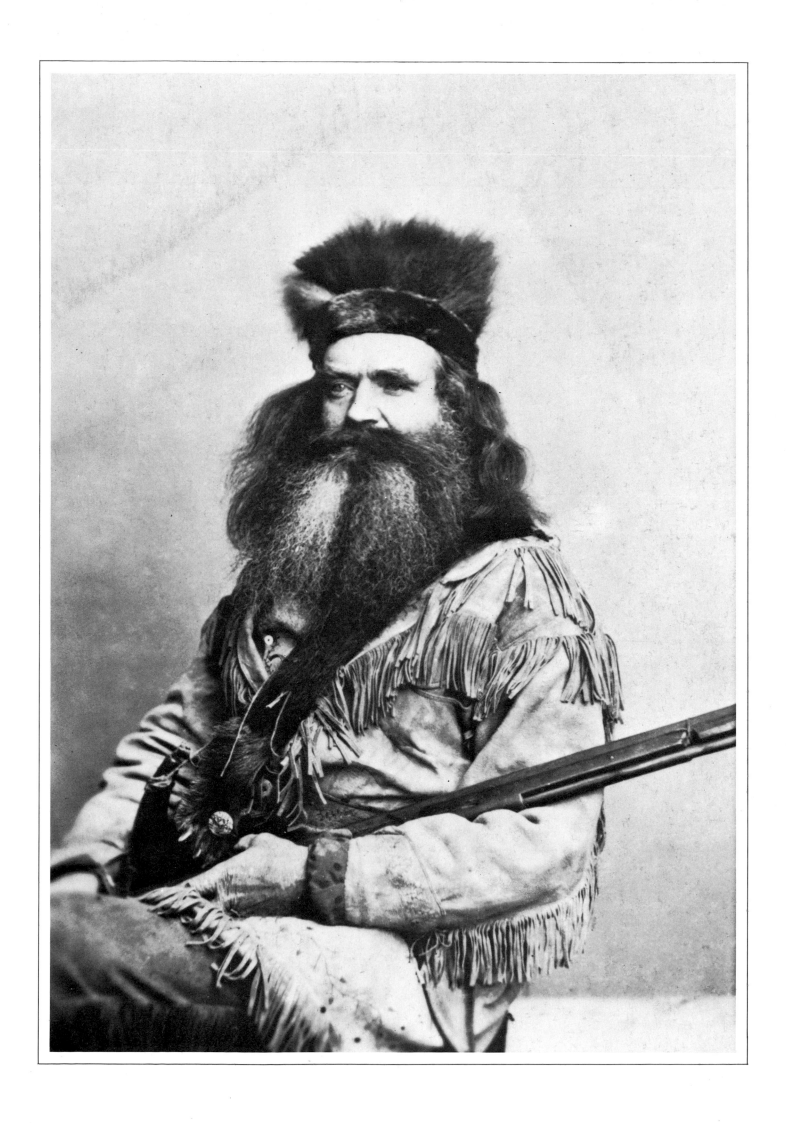

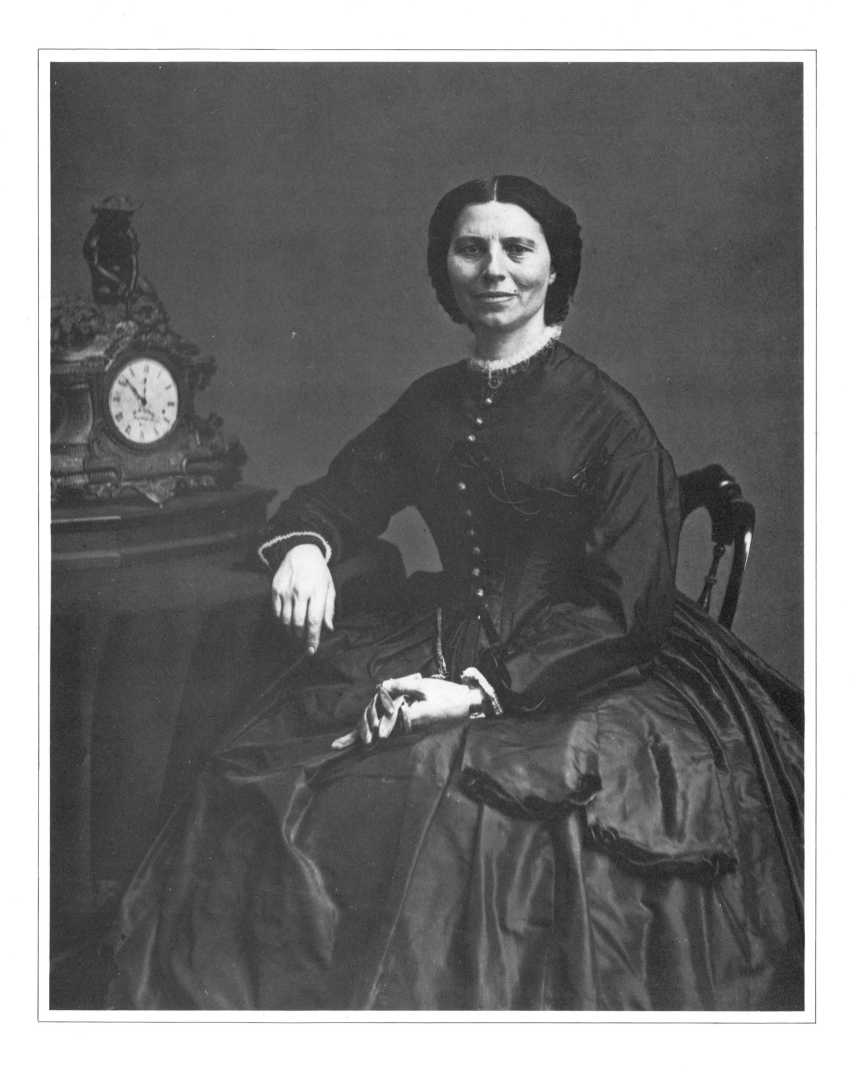

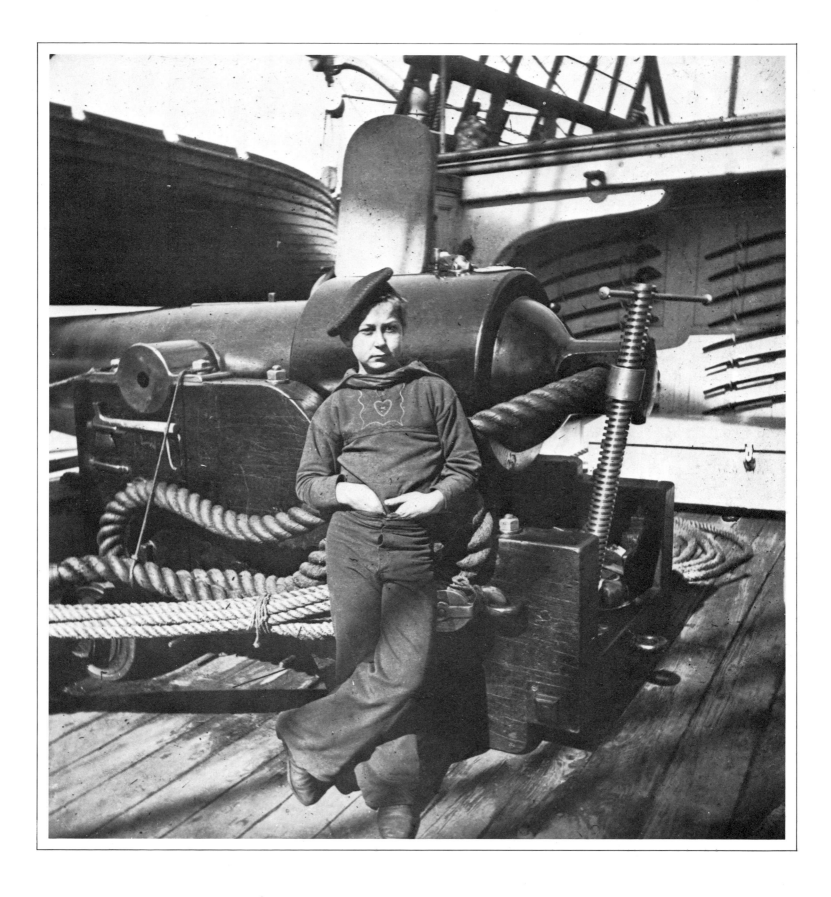

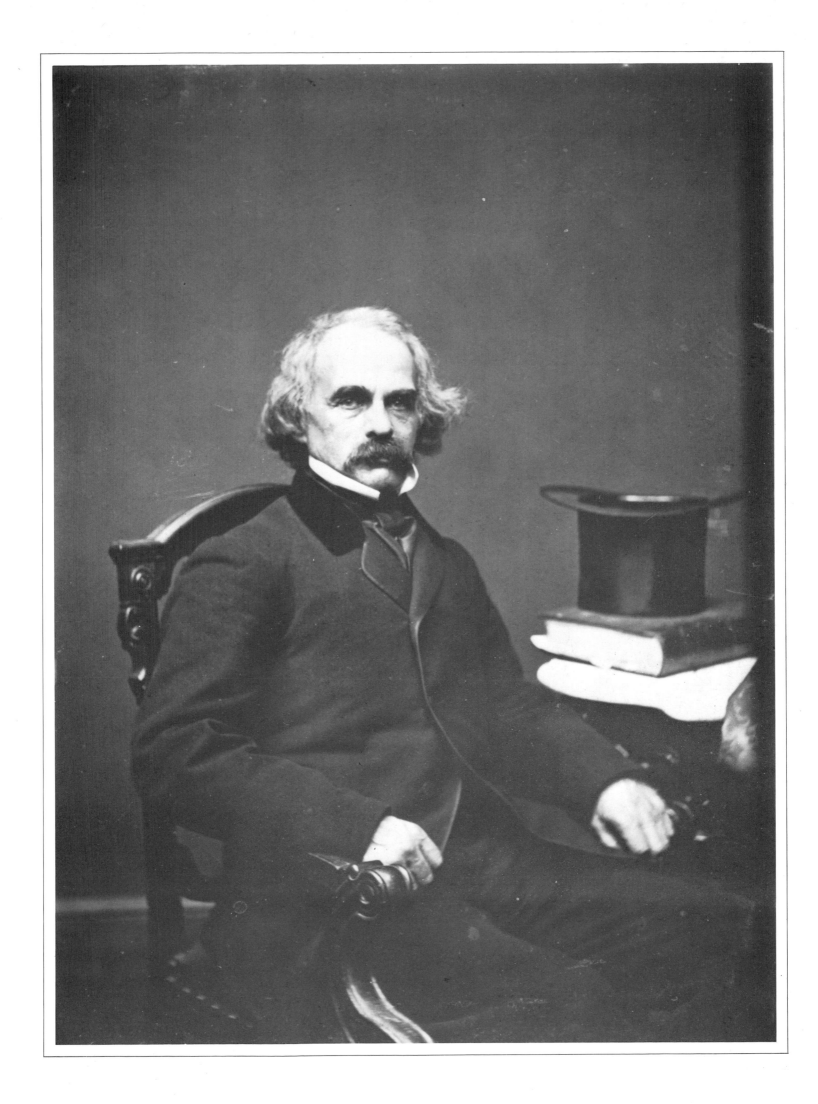

Nathaniel Hawthorne, 1862 (National Portrait Gallery, Washington, DC)

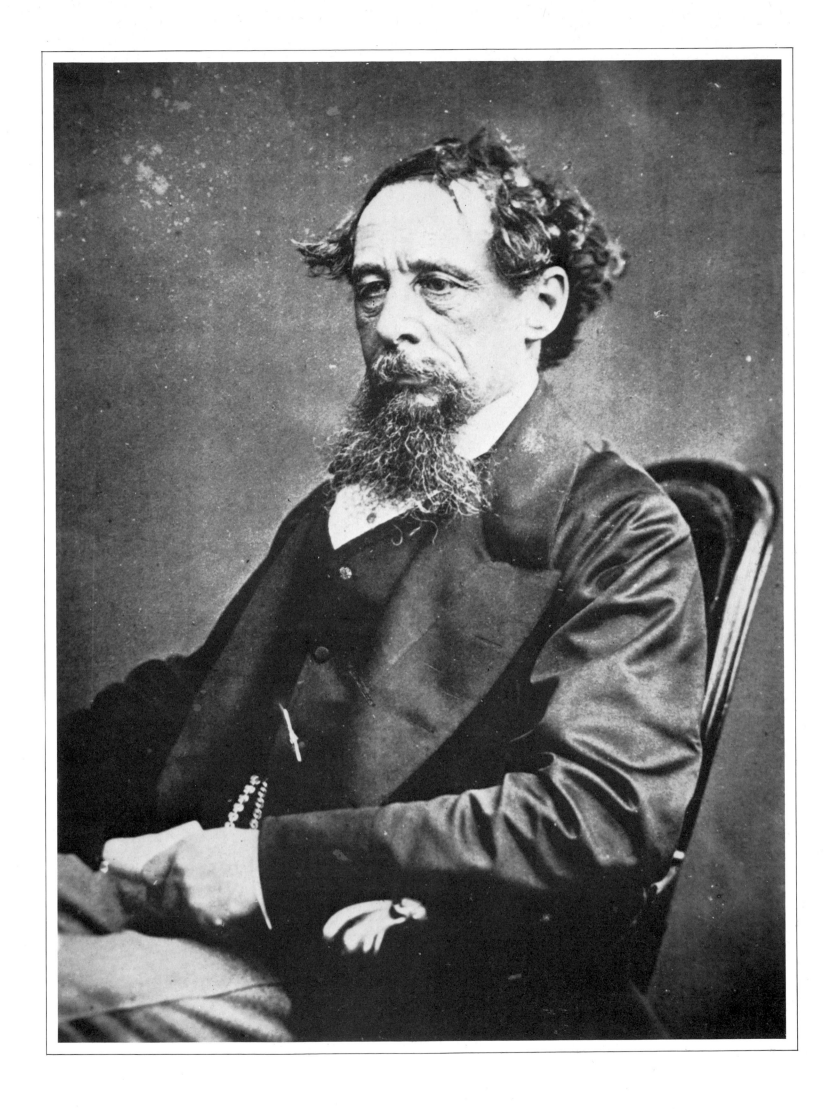

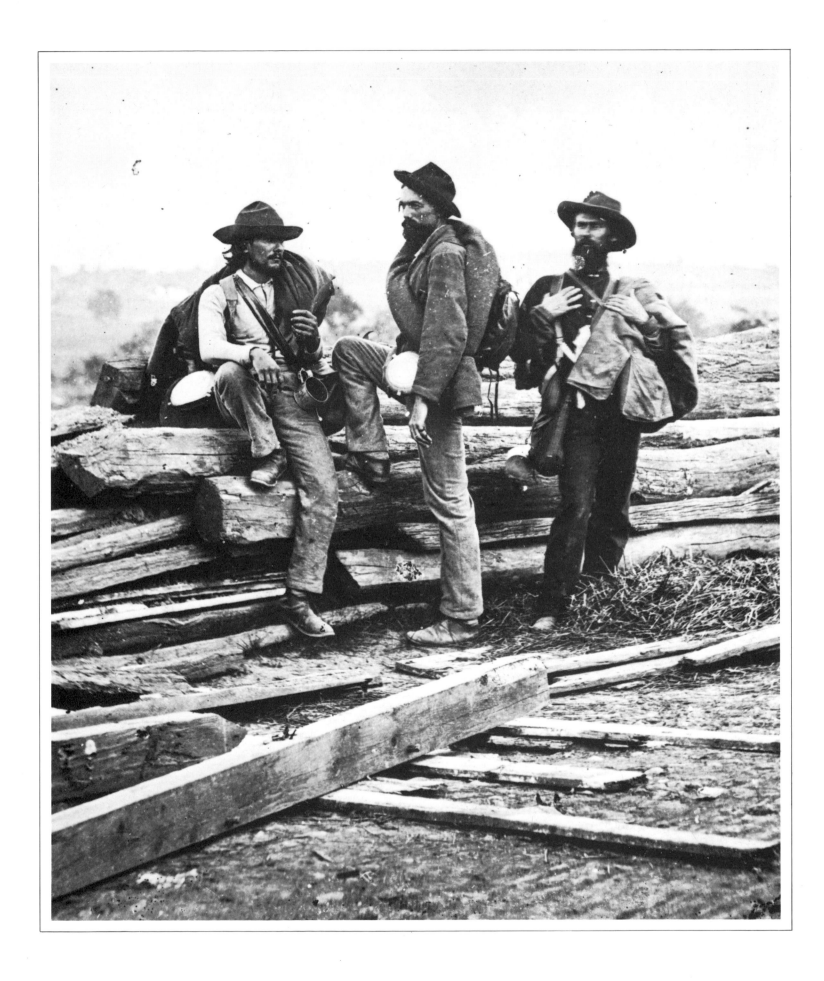

Three Confederate prisoners, Gettysburg, Pennsylvania, 1863 (Library of Congress, Washington, DC)

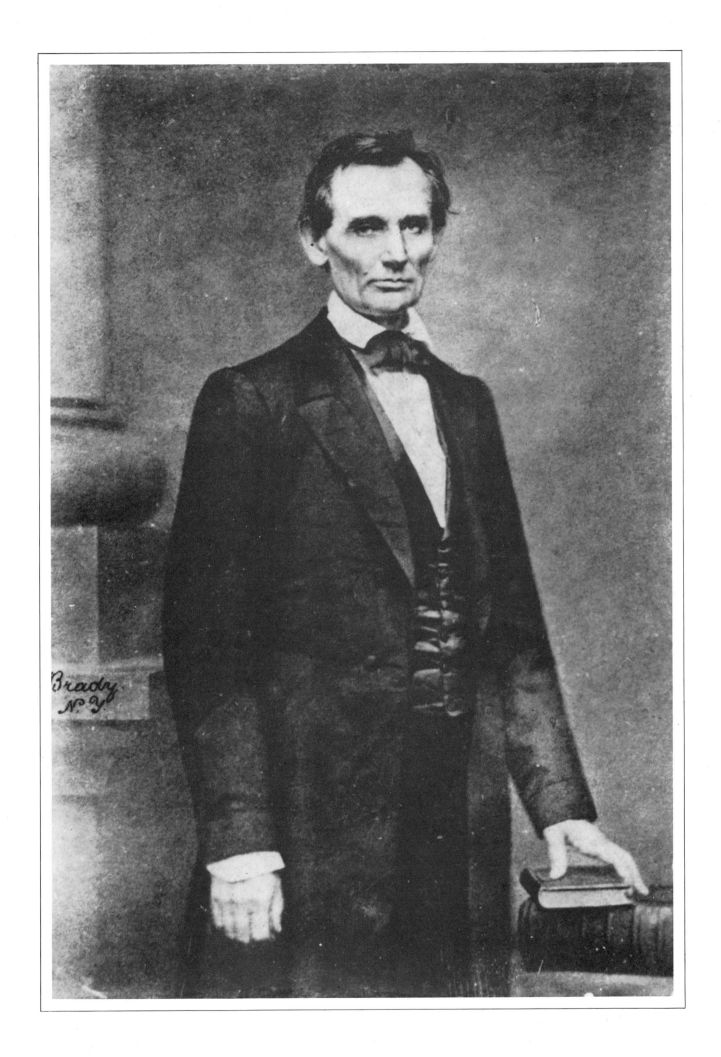

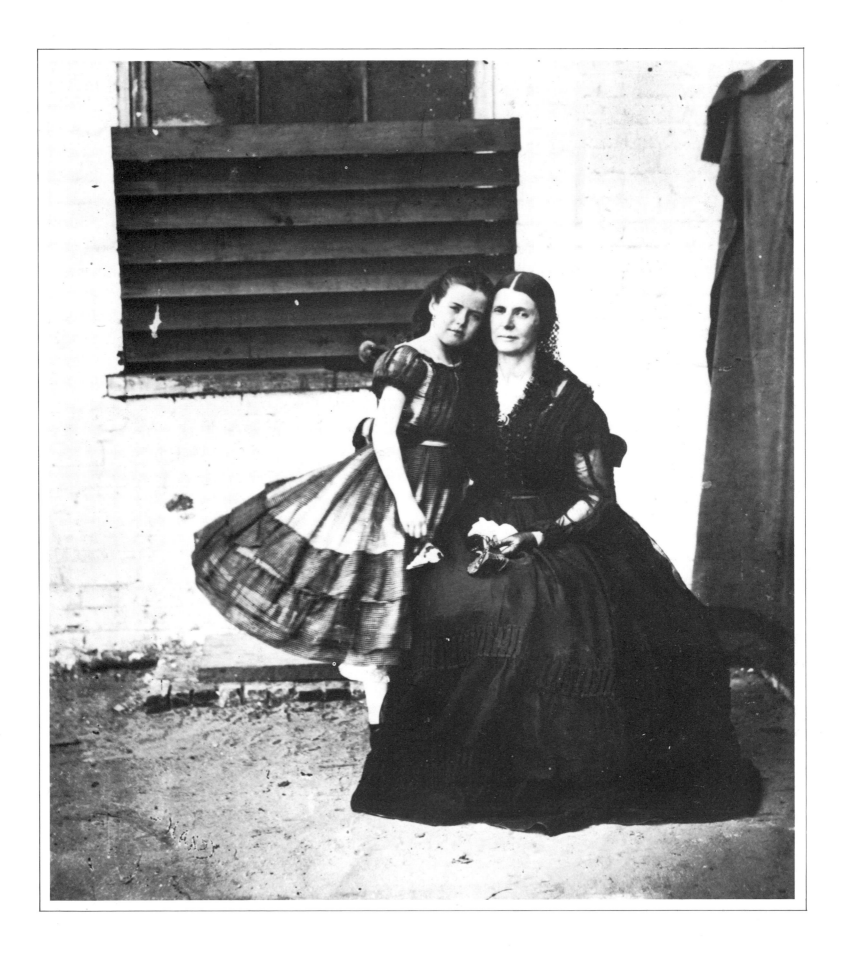

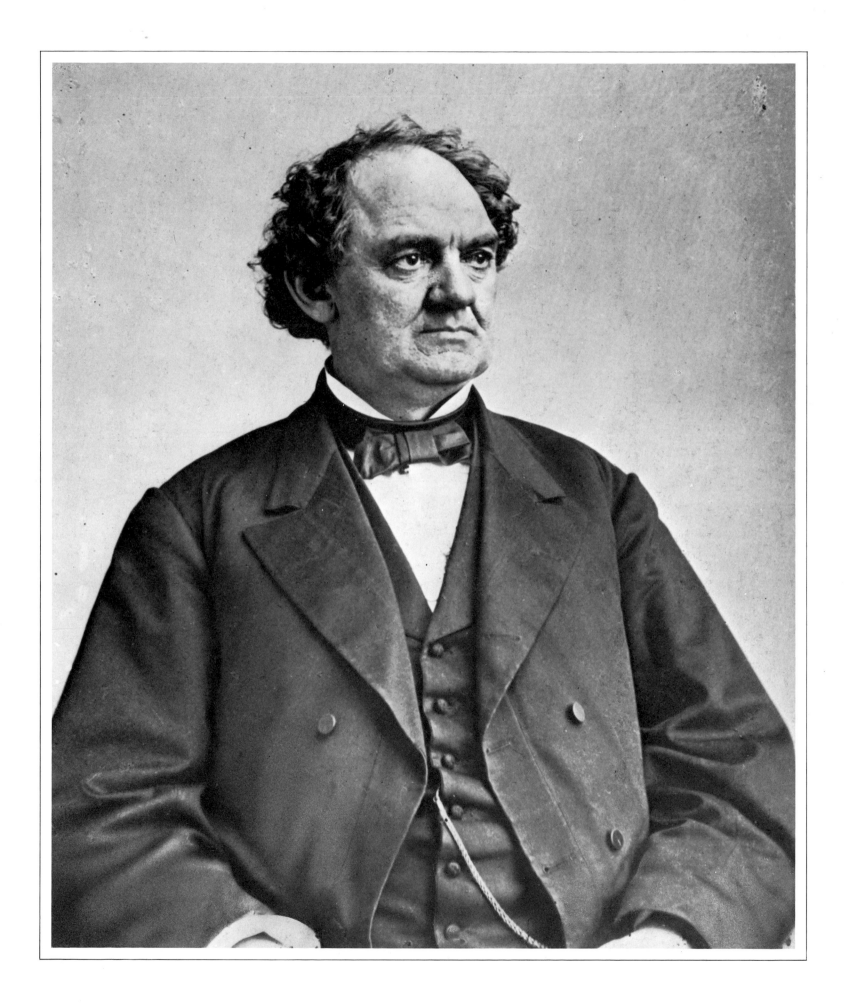

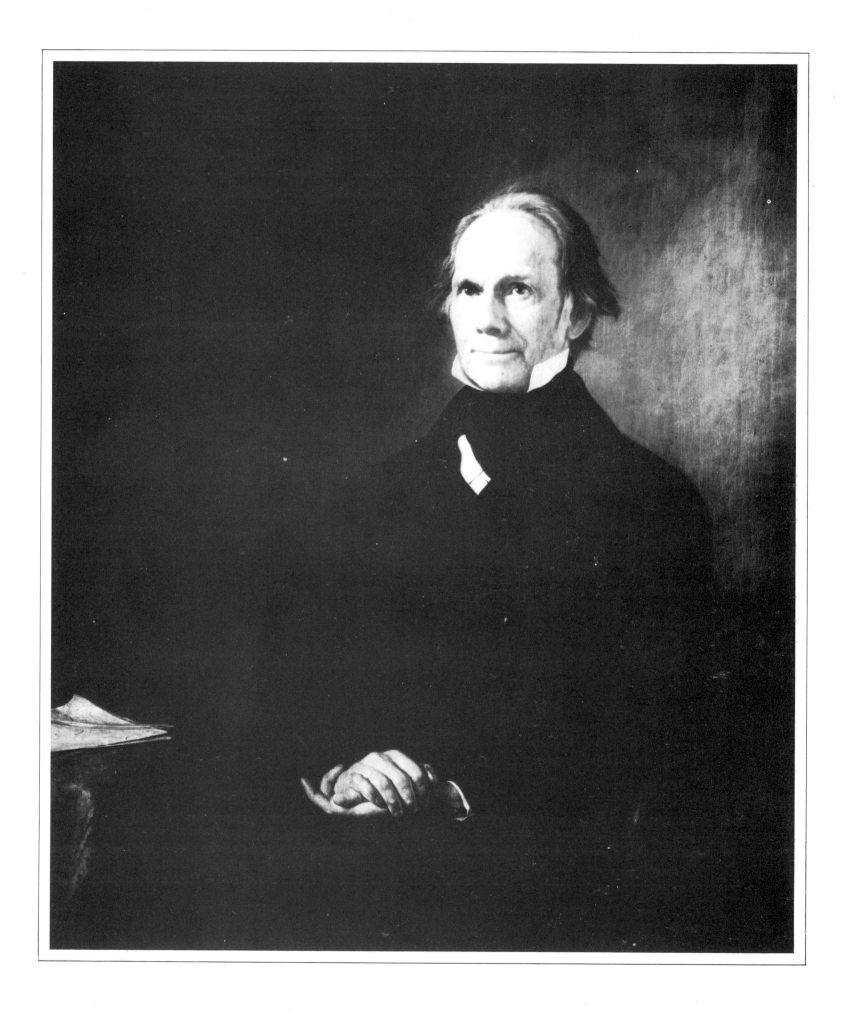

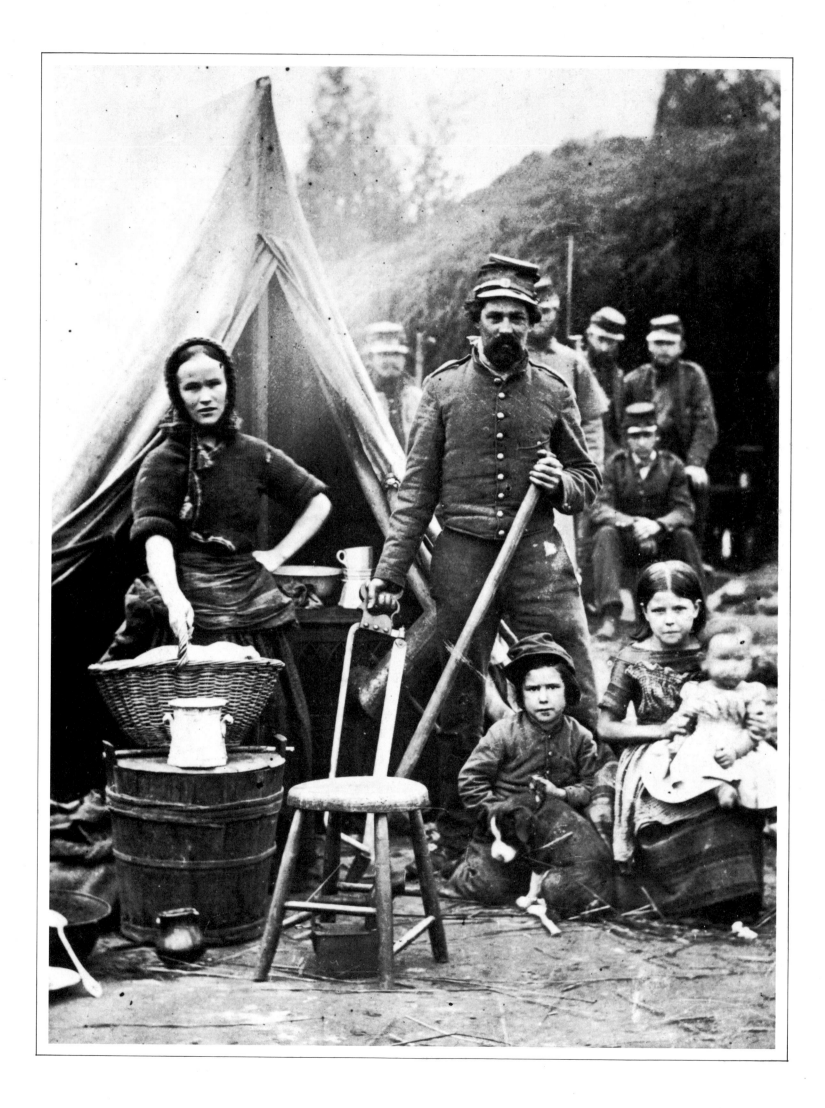

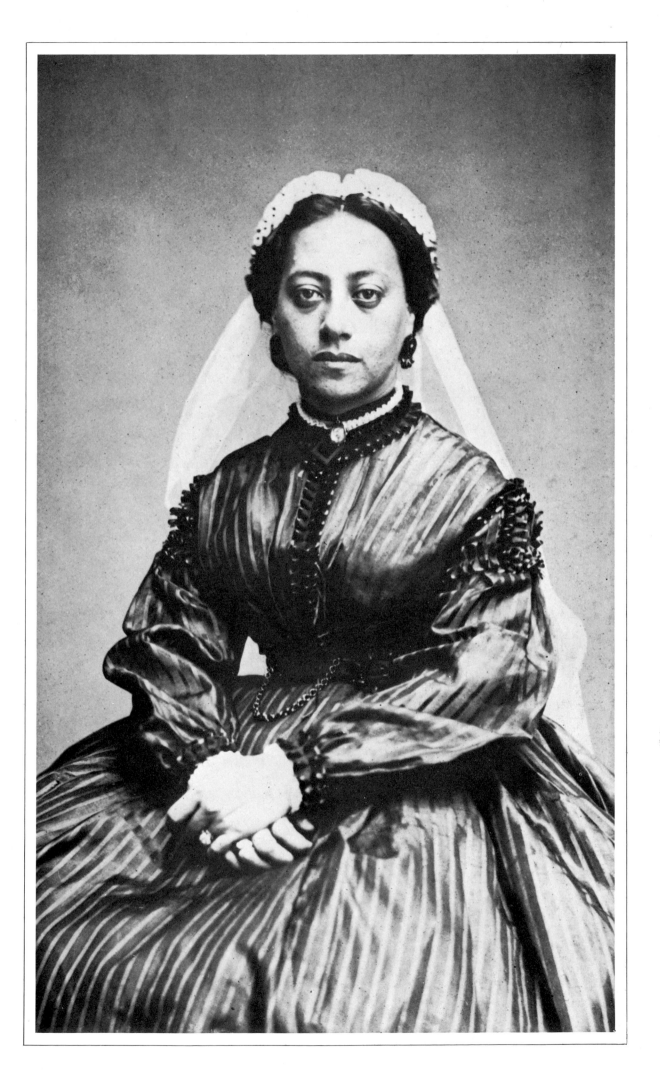

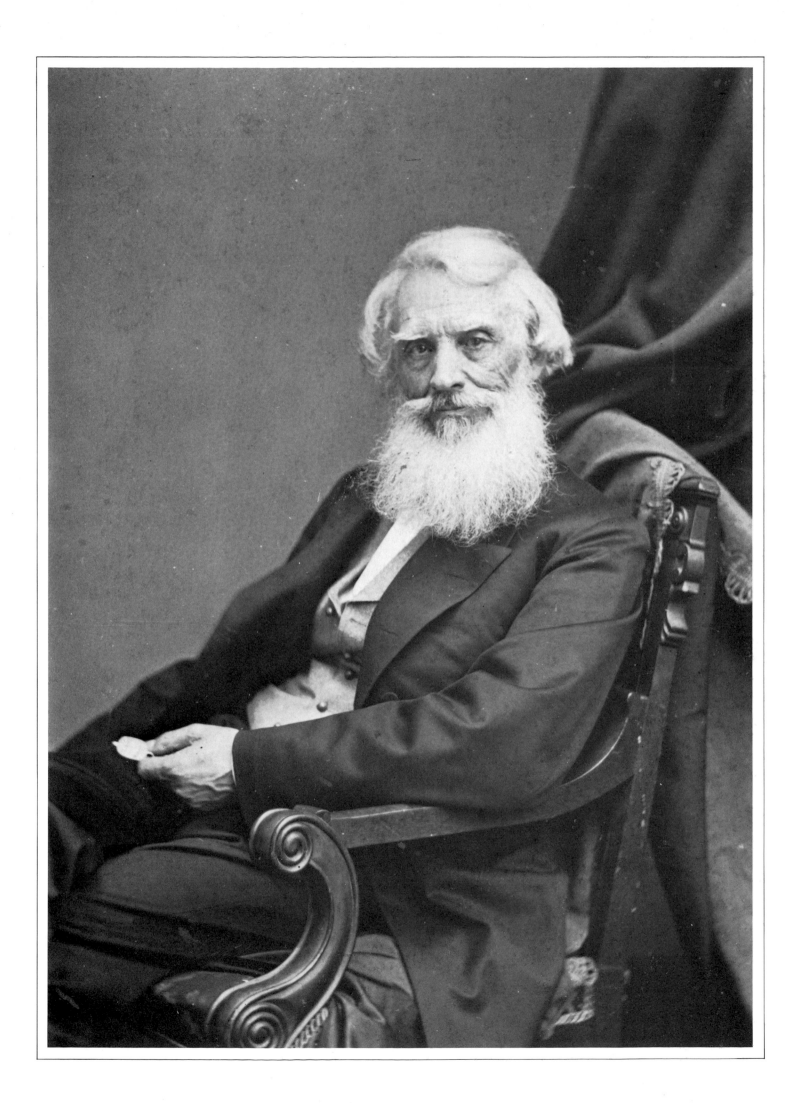

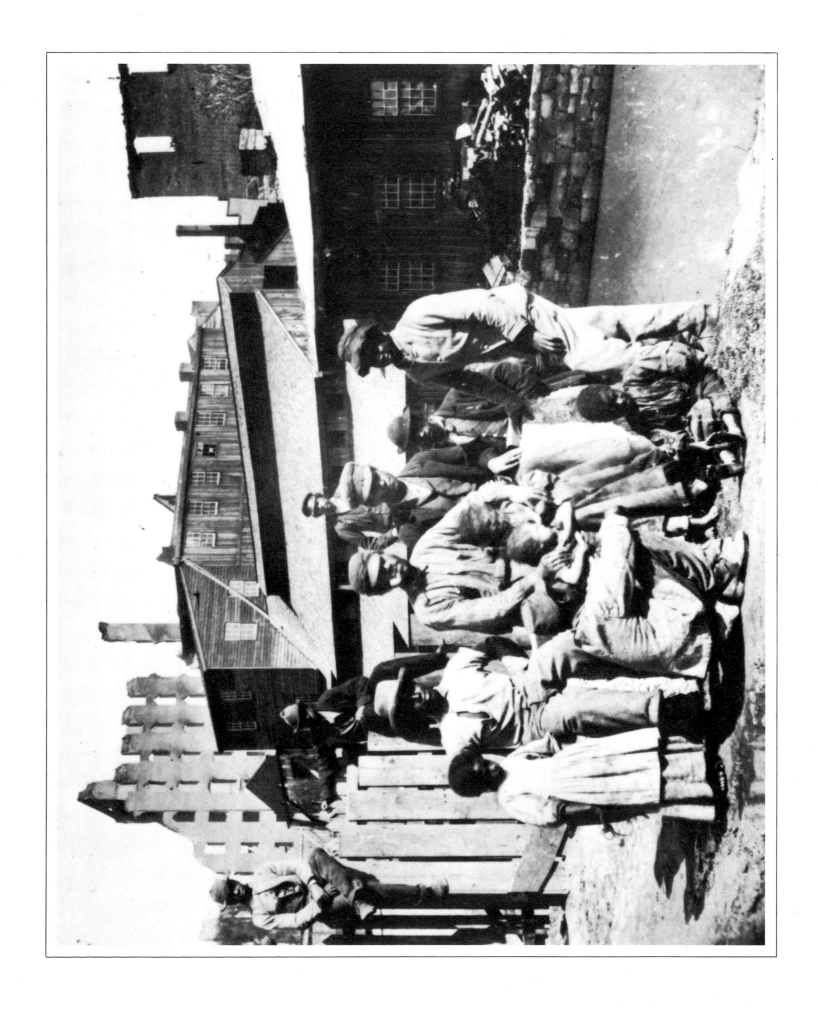

Freedmen on the canal bank at Richmond, Virginia, 1865 (Library of Congress, Washington, DC)

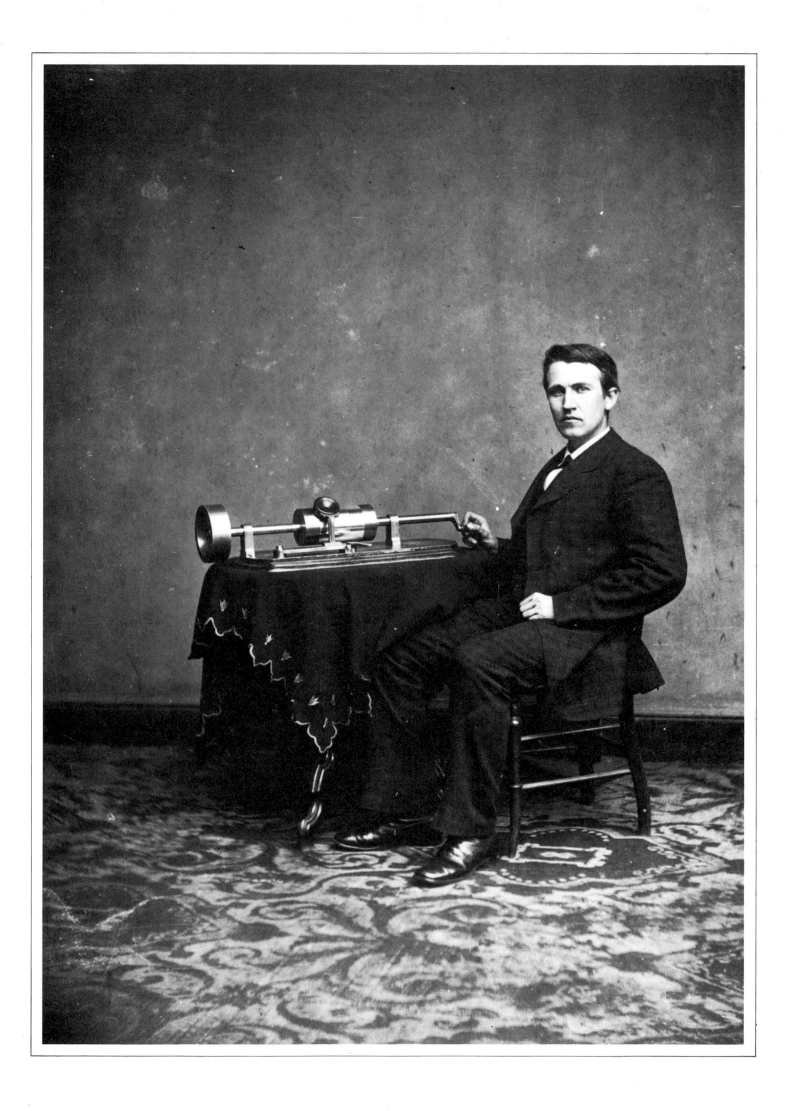

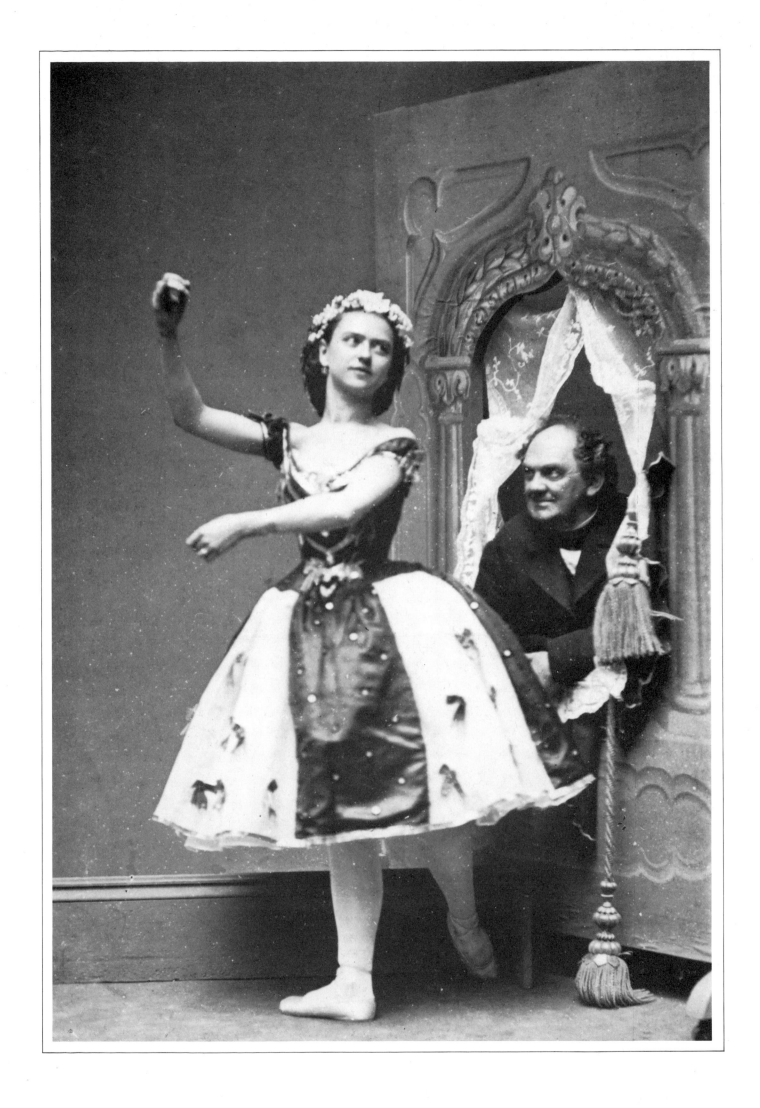

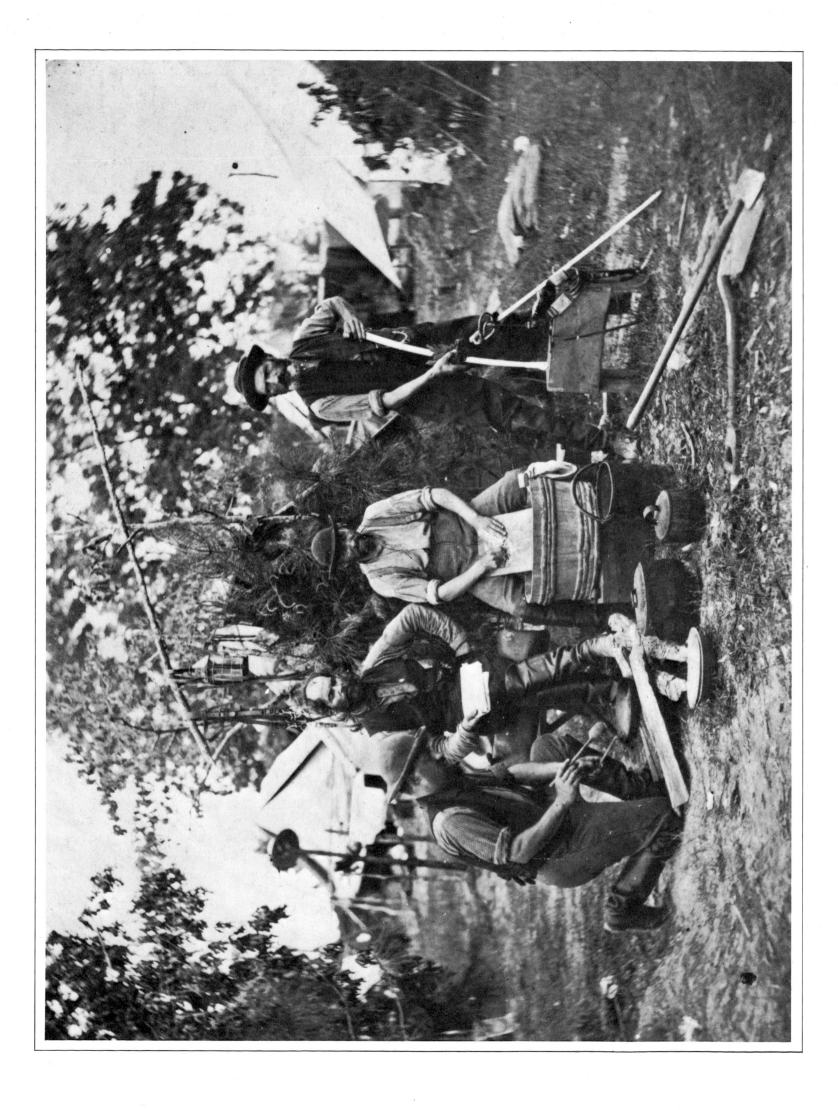

Camp work, vicinity of Yorktown, Virginia, 1862 (Library of Congress, Washington, DC)